KU-754-178

A Chocolate Bar

Sarah Ridley

W
FRANKLIN WATTS
LONDON·SYDNEY

First published in 2005 by
Franklin Watts
96 Leonard Street
London
EC2A 4XD

Franklin Watts Australia
45-51 Huntley Street
Alexandria, NSW 2015

© Franklin Watts 2005

ISBN: 0 7496 6062 7
Dewey classification number: 664.5

Series editor: Sarah Peutrill
Art director: Jonathan Hair
Design: Jemima Lumley

The Publisher and Author thank The Day Chocolate
Company for their help with this book.

A CIP catalogue record for this book is available
from the British Library.

Printed in Malaysia

Photo credits: AKG Images: 17c. Cadburys/News Team International: 21,
23c, 27bl, 27cr. The Day Chocolate Company: front cover cl, 1l, 5b, 7tr, 8,
19bl, 25t, 26tl, 26cl, 26bl, 27br. Fiona Duale/Divine Chocolate: front cover tl,
b, back cover t, 1r, 4t, 11b. Geri Engberd/Image Works/Topham: 24t. Mary
Evans Picture Library: 15b, 23b, 24b, 29. Owen Franken/Corbis: 20t, 27c.
Ron Giling/Still Pictures: 15t. Masterfoods: 11t, 22b, 27tr. Richard
Melloul/Sygma/Corbis: 18, 27tl. Ray Moller/Franklin Watts: 28. Brian
Moody: front cover c, 6b, 7bl, 7tl, 9tl, 10bl, 12t, 12b, 26tr. Museo de America,
Madrid/Dagli Orti/Art Archive: 9br. Museum of London/HIP/Topham:
20b. Kim Naylor: front cover cr, 14tr, 16t, 16b, 23tl, 25b, 26cr, 26br. Christine
Osborne/Ecoscene: 4c. Karen Robinson: back cover c, 6t, 10tr, 13t. Karen
Robinson/Panos: 31. Georgia Glynn-Smith/ABPL: 17t, 19tr, 27cl. Sven
Torfinn/Panos: 14bl. Mireille Vautier/Art Archive: 13b. Peter Wilson/Holt
Studios: 5t. Every attempt has been made to clear copyright. Should there
be any inadvertent omission please apply to the publisher for rectification.

Contents

4 Chocolate is made from cocoa beans.

6 When the pods are ripe, the farmers cut them down.

8 The pulp and the beans are piled onto leaves.

10 The farmers spread the beans on village drying tables.

12 The dried beans are put into sacks.

14 The cocoa beans go on a journey.

16 In the factory, the beans pass through many stages.

18 Rollers grind the cocoa nibs into a liquid.

20 The liquor is loaded into tankers.

22 The warm chocolate mixture is tempered.

24 The chocolate bar is checked.

26 How a Fairtrade chocolate bar is made

28 More ways to use cocoa

29 The original chocolate companies

30 Fairtrade and Kuapa Kokoo

32 Word bank

32 Index

Chocolate is made from cocoa beans.

▲ This milk chocolate bar contains cocoa, milk, sugar and vanilla.

Follow the story to see how the beans become a chocolate bar like this one. The story starts in Ghana, West Africa, where the beans grow inside pods on cacao trees.

▲ Cocoa beans grow inside a pod.

The beans are taken to Europe. In the Netherlands and then Germany they are made into chocolate.

► Most of the chocolate eaten in the UK is made from cocoa beans grown in Ghana. American chocolate bars are also made from cocoa grown in West Africa, as well as cocoa from Central and South America.

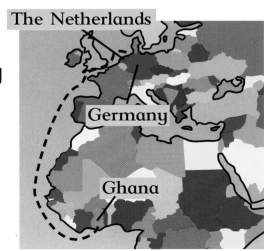

The Netherlands

Germany

Ghana

First the farmer prepares some land in the shade of some trees. He plants cacao seeds and the trees begin to grow. Cacao trees are often planted in rainforests or under banana or rubber trees.

Most cacao trees in Ghana grow on small family farms. Three to five years after planting the seeds, the trees burst into flower.

Cocoa pods develop from these flowers.

▲ Each tree produces about 10,000 tiny flowers, from which about 20 to 30 develop into cocoa pods.

▲ The cocoa beans inside the pods are the seeds of the cacao tree.

Where do cacao trees grow?

Cacao trees only grow near the Equator where the weather is always hot and wet. They originally grew in the rainforests of South America. Seeds were taken from there and planted in equatorial Africa, the Caribbean, Malaysia, Sri Lanka and Indonesia.

When the pods are ripe, the farmers cut them down.

Every year each tree produces between 20 to 30 pods, containing about 40 beans per pod. The pods turn yellow or orange when they are ripe. The green ones are left on the tree.

The farmer is careful not to harm the pods or the tree as he slices the ripe pods off.

▲ The farmer uses a sharp blade, or machete, to cut the pods off the tree.

The whole village joins in with the harvest, which happens twice a year.

◄ This woman is carrying harvested pods to a collection point.

Now the farmers cut the pods open.

▲ A close look inside a cocoa pod.

Inside there are damp white cocoa beans resting in pulp.

▲ The farmer splits the pods open with a sharp blade.

The pulp and the beans are carefully scraped out of the pods into baskets. At this point the cocoa beans taste very bitter. The pulp, however, tastes sweet.

◄ The pulp and the beans are kept together for the time being.

The pulp and the beans are piled onto leaves.

The farmers use dark green plantain leaves for this job. Plantains are a type of banana tree that often grow alongside cacao trees.

The farmers wrap the leaves around each heap of pulp and beans to create leaf parcels.

The parcels are left in the sun for between five and eight days.

◄ A heap of slimy beans and pulp.

Inside the leaf parcels it becomes really hot. The heat makes the pulp ferment, which means that bacteria and yeasts in the pulp multiply. This releases chemicals that change the flavour of the beans.

The pulp turns to liquid and drains out of the leaf parcels. The beans are taken out of the parcels.

◄ The leaf parcels are wrapped up tightly.

In the past

The Maya people lived in Central America, just south of where Mexico is today, from the 4th century CE. They are the first people to have left records of making a drink from cocoa beans. The Maya roasted, pounded and fermented the beans with maize and pepper. They called the beans *cacao* meaning, 'food of the gods'.

The Aztecs (see page 13) learned to make a chocolate drink from the Maya. They poured it from a height to make it frothy.

The farmers spread the beans on village drying tables.

It does not usually rain in Ghana at harvest time. This means that the beans can be left out in the open, on drying tables made from bamboo. The farmers take it in turns to turn the beans over.

➤ People turn the beans to help them dry, picking out any bad ones.

It takes between five and twelve days for the beans to dry.

◄ The beans are regularly checked for quality.

As the beans dry they shrink in size. Now they look very different from the damp white beans harvested from the pods two weeks earlier.

► The beans have shrunk because they have lost a lot of the water inside them.

What is Fairtrade chocolate?

This chocolate bar is made from fairly-traded cocoa beans. This means that the cocoa beans were grown under good working conditions. The farmers received a fair price for their cocoa beans and were sure of a buyer every time. Fairtrade farmers are not as poor as many cocoa farmers in the past, or in other parts of the world today. For more about Fairtrade, see page 30.

Fairtrade chocolate companies make many types of chocolate.

The dried beans are put into sacks.

▲ ► The sacks are filled and sewn up.

The beans are sorted so that the beans in each bag are the same quality. The farmer and his family have done everything so far, from planting the seeds to sewing up the bean sacks. Now they can sell the beans.

The farmer's sacks are checked for quality and weighed. This is done by a man called a recorder. He also arranges for lorries to collect the sacks.

For now the recorder pays the farmer half the value of each sack, making sure he pays a fair price. The recorder pays the farmer the other half after the sacks have been sold to Cocobod (see next page).

▲ The village recorder checks the weight of each sack and keeps careful records.

In the past

Today the price of cocoa beans can vary. The Aztecs, who settled in Central America from the 14th century, used the beans like we use money. Four cocoa beans could buy a pumpkin, 10 cocoa beans equalled a rabbit (to eat!) and 100 beans bought a slave.

Aztecs offer Hernadez Cortez (see page 17), an honoured visitor, their much-valued cocoa drink.

The cocoa beans go on a journey.

First the sacks of beans are loaded onto lorries.

➤ It takes two men to load each sack because they weigh 62 kilograms!

▼ Cargo ships can carry hundreds of sacks.

The full lorry is driven to the capital of Ghana, Accra. Here the government cocoa board, Cocobod, buys all the sacks of beans. As the farmers belong to a farmers' cooperative (see page 31), they get a better price for their cocoa beans than other farmers. Now the sacks are loaded onto cargo ships, which set sail for Europe.

The sacks of dry, hard cocoa beans arrive in the Netherlands for the next stage.

▲ Men pile up the sacks of cocoa beans once they arrive at the port in the Netherlands.

Why do the beans go to the Netherlands?

In 1828 a Dutchman named Conraad Van Houten invented a machine that could press 50% of the cocoa butter out of the beans to leave dry cocoa cakes and rich cocoa butter. Although some chocolate companies, especially in the USA, have built their own cocoa presses, much cocoa is still pressed in the Netherlands, or in Germany.

An early advert for Van Houten cocoa powder, 'The best of all the drinking chocolate'.

In the factory, the beans pass through many stages.

The workers split open the sacks and pour the beans into a sorting machine. This sorts out the different sizes of bean and cleans them.

➤ The factory workers often mix sacks of different types of cocoa bean to get a good-tasting chocolate mixture.

Then the beans are roasted at a high temperature to improve the flavour further and to kill any harmful micro-organisms.

◀ The beans are roasted for between 10 and 35 minutes at temperatures of 120°C or more.

Now the cocoa beans are so brittle that the next machines can break them open and blow away the shells with jets of air. This is called winnowing and it leaves just the cocoa nibs.

➤ The leftover bean shells are removed.

In the past

How did chocolate spread to Europe?

Christopher Columbus and Hernandez Cortez were European explorers working for Spain in the early 16th century.

Columbus bought back a few cocoa beans to Spain in 1502 but it was Cortez who saw the value of the cocoa bean. In 1528 he brought back a cargo of cocoa beans from Central America with the tools to make the chocolate drink. It became very popular in Spain and from there spread to the rest of Europe.

When Columbus landed on Guanaja, Central America, in 1502, Aztecs brought him gifts including a sack of cocoa beans.

Rollers grind the cocoa nibs into a liquid.

This brown liquid is called cocoa liquor and it has a very strong chocolate flavour. The liquor flows off the machine into shallow containers.

Some of the cocoa liquor leaves the factory at this point to go to the chocolate factory. The rest goes through another stage.

Cocoa liquor contains a fat called cocoa butter. This butter is squeezed out of the leftover cocoa liquor using a powerful machine.

▲ Rollers squash the nibs and turn them into a brown liquid.

What is left is solid cakes of cocoa powder called presscakes, and cocoa butter. The cocoa butter is used to help make chocolate, as well as soap and skin creams.

The presscakes are ground down into a powder. This is then sold as cocoa for hot drinks, or used to flavour cakes, biscuits or ice cream.

▲ Trays of finely ground cocoa powder wait to be put into tins.

▲ It takes up to a year's crop of cocoa beans from one tree to make one tin of cocoa powder.

In the past

How did chocolate get its name?

When the Spanish arrived in Central America (see page 17), where Mexico is today, they met the Aztecs. The Aztecs offered the Spanish a drink made from cocoa beans that they called *chocol haa*, meaning 'hot drink'. South of the Aztecs, the Maya used the word *chokola'j*, which meant 'to drink chocolate together'. Back in Europe people called the drink *chocolat* and then finally chocolate.

The liquor is loaded into tankers.

The cocoa tankers set off for the chocolate factory in Germany. Now the final stage of the chocolate production begins. The cocoa butter is added to the cocoa liquor. The extra cocoa butter makes the chocolate softer and more 'melt in the mouth'.

▲ Cocoa butter is poured into the cocoa liquor.

A scene inside a chocolate house in 1787.

In the past

Drinking hot chocolate was a popular pastime for rich people in 17th century European cities. Some people drank it at home but there were also chocolate houses. These were like clubs where men and women could chat or do business. At the time poor people could not afford hot chocolate. In the 19th century the price of powdered cocoa came down and then everyone could enjoy hot chocolate.

Sugar, vanilla and powdered or evaporated milk are also added at this stage. Now all the ingredients are mixed together.

The whole mixture is put through another series of rollers to mix everything up and make it really smooth.

Next the conching begins. This is when the chocolate mixture is stirred constantly at a warm temperature for a day or more. Gradually the chocolate develops an incredibly smooth texture and an even better flavour.

▲ All the ingredients of the chocolate bar are mixed in a huge machine.

The warm chocolate mixture is tempered.

The mixture flows into tempering kettles. These are large metal containers. In the tempering kettles, paddles keep the chocolate moving as it is carefully warmed and cooled.

▼ This chocolate has become very shiny and smooth after tempering.

The factory workers take great care as the chocolate could be ruined at this stage. Finally, when they are sure that the chocolate is ready, they push a button to let it flow into moulds.

◄ The factory worker tests the chocolate to see if it is ready.

In the past

The first true chocolate bar was made in England by J S Fry in 1847. He added some cocoa butter to a mixture of cocoa powder and sugar to make a chocolate bar. At first, only the rich could afford such a treat as it was expensive.

An advert for Fry's chocolate from 1907.

▼ The chocolate runs into the mould.

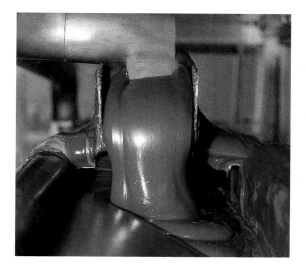

The chocolate is now cooled in its moulds. When it is cold the bars are tipped out onto a conveyor belt.

The chocolate bar is checked.

The factory worker checks the bars of chocolate, to make sure they are all good enough to sell.

◀ As the conveyor belt passes before her eyes, the factory worker looks for poor quality chocolate bars.

Is chocolate good for you?

Chocolate can be good for you as long as you don't eat too much! It is high in fat and sugar so it could make you put on weight. However, scientists have discovered that chocolate, especially dark chocolate, contains chemicals that can protect your heart against disease and help to prevent cancer.

In the past, chocolate companies were allowed to advertise chocolate as a healthy food.

CHOC-FULL OF GOODNESS !

Now machines wrap each bar in foil and put the paper wrapper on. Bars of chocolate are packed in boxes and then into lorries, which take them to shops in the UK to sell them. Some bars are also shipped abroad to countries such as the USA and Canada.

▶ It takes a whole crop of beans from just one tree to make between four and six bars of chocolate like this!

◀ The chocolate bars finally reach the shops. There are a huge range of chocolate bars to choose from. This is another Fairtrade chocolate bar.

How a Fairtrade chocolate bar is made

1. The cocoa pods grow on the cacao tree.

4. The farmers spread the beans out on drying tables.

2. The farmers harvest the ripe pods and split them open.

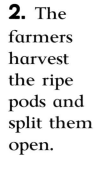

5. The beans are shipped to a cocoa processing factory in the Netherlands.

3. The pulp and beans are wrapped in leaf parcels and left to ferment.

6. Machines clean, roast and winnow the beans, leaving cocoa nibs.

7. The cocoa nibs are squashed to form cocoa liquor.

11. Next the chocolate is conched and then tempered, stirring all the time as it is warmed and cooled.

8. Some cocoa liquor goes through a press to extract cocoa butter, leaving cocoa powder.

12. The warm chocolate flows into moulds, where it is cooled and tipped out as bars.

9. In the German chocolate factory, the cocoa butter is added to the cocoa liquor.

10. Milk, sugar and cocoa butter are added to the mixture.

13. The bars are wrapped and packed, ready to eat.

More ways to use cocoa

How many ways have you eaten chocolate?

Chocolate shapes

Chocolate muffin

Chocolate ice cream

Chocolate roll

Chocolate biscuits

Chocolate only uses the cocoa nibs at the centre of the cocoa bean. Many other products use the rest of the cocoa pod.
Here are just a few:

➤ the husks of the pod are used to make animal feed. They are also used to make soap and fertiliser

➤ the pulp juice is collected during fermentation and bottled to be sold as drinks

➤ cocoa shells are used by gardeners to improve the soil

➤ cocoa butter is used in moisturising creams for the skin and for soaps.

The original chocolate companies

Many of today's chocolate companies in England and the USA were set up by people who felt they should look after their workers. This was at a time when many working people suffered bad working conditions and poor housing.

▲ The housing and environment of Bournville were much better than workers were used to.

New towns

In 1879 George Cadbury of the Cadbury chocolate company built a new factory, called Bournville, near Birmingham in the UK. He then built a village for his workers, including houses, shops and schools.

Other chocolate companies, like Rowntree and Terry's of York, also built houses, schools and training colleges.

In the USA, Milton Hershey built the factory town of Hershey in Pennsylvania. He then built a zoo and an amusement park for his workers' entertainment!

Fairtrade and Kuapa Kokoo

Fairtrade

You may have noticed the Fairtrade label on some of the food you eat. You can buy Fairtrade bananas, tea, rice, honey, coffee and many other products as well as chocolate. Most of these goods are grown in the poorer parts of the world.

Kuapa Kokoo

Kuapa Kokoo is the name for a group of Ghanaian cocoa farmers who have joined together to form a cooperative. It means 'good cocoa farmers' in Twi - the local language. Their motto is 'PaPa Paa' which means 'the best of the best'.

Fairtrade labels

The Fairtrade label means that:

➤ the farmers receive a fair, fixed price for their goods

➤ the cocoa buyers pay a 'social premium'. This means the community receives money for improvements such as healthcare and water

➤ the farmers have long-term contracts with the buyers of their goods

➤ the farmers work in good conditions and have a say in how the organisation runs.

Different countries have their own Fairtrade labels, e.g:

 UK

Look for this label on Fairtrade products

USA and Canada

Find out more about Fairtrade at: www.fairtrade.org.uk

Working together

The cooperative works for the good of all its 45,000 members to help them grow and sell their cocoa beans. All the cocoa sold by Kuapa Kokoo is grown under Fairtrade conditions.

The Day Chocolate Company

Kuapa Kokoo owns one third of The Day Chocolate Company, which makes Dubble and Divine chocolate bars. Extra money made by the company is shared among the farmers who grew the cocoa in Ghana.

◀ Most cocoa farmers earn £125 per year in total.

The benefits of belonging to Kuapa Kokoo:
➤ the farmers earn more as a cooperative because they have better selling power and are more efficient at doing business
➤ at the end of the year, any profit made by the cooperative is divided up and paid as a bonus to each farmer
➤ Kuapa Kokoo pays for improvements to villages, such as better water supplies
➤ Kuapa Kokoo buys many tools at once, at a lower price, which they can sell on to their members
➤ Kuapa Kokoo organises training and education.

Word bank

Bacteria The name for many different types of very small single-celled living things that live everywhere.

Conching Part of the chocolate-making process. The conching machine stirs the warm mixture to develop a smooth flavour and texture.

Conveyor belt A constantly moving belt of rubber used in factories to move things about.

Cooperative A group of people who join together to work for a better life for them all, including better prices or better working conditions.

Ferment To make something bubble up or start to break down, often using yeast (see below).

Micro-organisms Tiny microscopic living things, some of which cause illness.

Tempering Part of the chocolate-making process. By constantly stirring, heating and cooling the chocolate mixture, it develops a shiny appearance and an even better flavour.

Yeast A group of tiny fungi that use sugar to grow. When yeast grows in cocoa leaf parcels, the pulp and beans ferment to develop the cocoa's flavour.

Index

Aztec 9, 13, 17, 19

cacao tree 4, 5, 6, 8, 19, 25, 26
Cadbury 29
Central America 4, 9, 13, 17, 19
chocolate
    bar 4, 11, 21, 23, 24, 25, 27, 31
    drink 9, 13, 15, 17, 19, 20
cocoa
    butter 15, 18, 19, 20, 23, 27, 28
    liquor 18, 20, 26
    nib 17, 18, 26, 27, 28
    pod 4, 5, 6, 7, 11, 26, 28

powder 15, 19, 20, 23, 27
pulp 7, 8, 9, 26, 28
cocoa bean
    drying 10-11, 26
    harvest 6-7, 10, 26
    planting 5, 12
    roast 16, 26
    selling 12, 13, 14, 30, 31
    winnow 17, 26
    wrap in parcels 8-9, 26
conching 21, 27
Cortez, H 13, 17

Day Chocolate Company, The 20, 27, 31

Fairtrade 11, 25, 26, 30-31

Germany 4, 15, 20, 27
Ghana 4, 5, 10, 14, 31

Hershey 29

Maya 9, 19

Netherlands 4, 15, 26

South America 4, 5
Spain 17, 19

tempering 22, 27

THE MAGICAL HISTORY OF
Unicorns

Publisher and Creative Director: Nick Wells

Senior Project Editor: Catherine Taylor

Art Director & Layout Deign: Mike Spender

Digital Design & Production: Chris Herbert

Copy Editor: Anna Groves

Special thanks to: Laura Bulbeck, Josie Mitchell, Josh Vitchkoski

and the artists who allowed us to reproduce their work

FLAME TREE PUBLISHING

6 Melbray Mews, Fulham,

London SW6 3NS, United Kingdom

www.flametreepublishing.com

First published 2017

(Artwork © respective contributors – *see* page 127)

17 19 21 20 18

1 3 5 7 9 10 8 6 4 2

ISBN 978-1-78664-531-9

A CIP record for this book is available from the British Library upon request.

Printed in China

THE MAGICAL HISTORY OF
Unicorns

Russ Thorne

FOREWORD BY REFFELIA

**FLAME TREE
PUBLISHING**

CONTENTS

Foreword 6

Introduction 8

Myth and Magic 14

Faith and Legend 28

Real Unicorns 40

Medical Marvels 48

War Horse 56

Artful Creatures 64

Bookish Beasts 84

Superstars of the Screen 104

Unicorns, Updated 118

Resources 124

Acknowledgments 126

FOREWORD

I believe that a world without fantasy is a cruel world to live in. Maybe that is why as an artist, I love fantasy themes, because they allow you to dream of a universe that we can't reach physically. Within the pages of this book, you will encounter the most pure being among all fantastical creatures – the unicorn.

Unicorns are wild creatures that symbolize hope and magic when the world falls into darkness, corruption and despair; children often dream about them. These unique beasts are usually associated with the celestial world, the moon and serenity. Present in old tales, myths and legends, it is said that only a few, with a pure heart, are likely to see them.

Perhaps it is the unicorns' innocence and purity that draw us to them, or their majestic ways of enchantment and calmness – they

can be our spiritual beacons. When you feel lost, and sadness surrounds you, like a cold, dark, dense forest, keep searching for the ray of light that shines upon you. It is there, if you keep looking for it, and never give up.

In art, it is that feeling between sorrow and resolution that the unicorns inspire in us. For me, they represent the tears that I don't shed when I am mourning a past that is beyond reach, hoping for a better tomorrow. These feelings are difficult to express verbally, but easier to depict in wonderful imagery, where the unicorns stand beautiful and unique, described by the singularity of each illustration, which I invite you all to see.

REFFELIA

reffelia.deviantart.com

INTRODUCTION

The world is full of unicorns. You can sip from your unicorn mug, while wearing your unicorn slippers and wearing your unicorn pyjamas. (Maybe you're doing that right now, in which case, you're in the right place.)

While you're doing it, you can cuddle up to your giant unicorn soft toy and watch the unicorn canter through films, TV shows and cartoons; or maybe read one of the many, many unicorn-inspired novels. The unicorn has wandered into almost every corner of popular culture – but it didn't do it overnight.

Magnetic Myths

Like so many mythical creatures, the unicorn has a long and turbulent past.

It's been on the Earth for as long as we have – or, depending on whom you believe, even longer. And like some of its mythical brothers and sisters – vampires, witches, fairies, mermaids – it has a peculiar hold on us.

We've told tales of the unicorn through folk stories, legends, art and literature for thousands of years, and its appeal seems to just be getting stronger. Maybe as the world embraces technology and sprints ahead, the stronger the desire becomes to look back, to slow down, to uncover a little magic beneath the mayhem.

What Does a Unicorn Look Like?

It seems like a simple enough question. Google 'unicorn' and hundreds of millions of similar images come up. Bring up the unicorn emoji and it's much the same. The covers of books, magical cards, calendars, anything remotely 'unicorn' show us the unicorn we probably all have in our heads: a white horse with a long, straight horn on its forehead, perhaps sporting some other colours on its mane and the horn itself. It might have wings, but generally not.

'I thought unicorns were more … fluffy.'
TERRY PRATCHETT, *LORDS AND LADIES*

But the unicorn of early legends was a very different animal.

Our Quest

In fact, those early legends talk of ferocious creatures, capable of killing men with ease and happy to do so. Some were huge, ugly and brutish. Others were small and deer-like. You couldn't tame them, or even get near them.

So how did we get from those creatures to pink, fluffy unicorns? And why do we love them so? Our quest is to find out. It's a long and magical

tale that says as much about us as it does about the unicorn. Along the way we'll meet monsters, knights, lovers, a goat that bowed before the most powerful man in the world, and Lady Gaga.

And like all good magical stories, it begins a long time ago and a long way away....

'The unicorn lived in a lilac wood, and she lived all alone. She was very old, though she did not know it, and she was no longer the careless color of sea foam but rather the color of snow falling on a moonlit night. But her eyes were still clear and unwearied, and she still moved like a shadow on the sea.'

PETER S. BEAGLE, *THE LAST UNICORN*

MYTH AND MAGIC

Where does the unicorn of your imagination live? Perhaps in an enchanted forest, or standing placidly in a glade near a magical pool. Or maybe it's a beast of wide open spaces and rolling plains, a sort of mythical mustang roaming wild and free. It could be the noble steed of a fantasy hero, or the companion of a magician.

It could be all, or none, of the above. The unicorn appears to each of us in its own way. And given its origins, it's not surprising that we might not agree on exactly what a unicorn might be like. We'll start our journey with a look at those origins.

The Missing Myth

Here's the thing about unicorns: it's not where we find them that's intriguing, but

where we *don't* find them. We're talking about a horned, magical being with powers that range from purifying water to healing wounds and removing poison, so surely there's bound to be a few of them knocking around in the stables of Greek mythology? After all, these tales are the origins of the flying horse Pegasus, Cerberus the three-headed dog, the one-eyed cyclops Polyphemus and snake-haired gorgon Medusa. A unicorn would be in fine company. But the unicorn doesn't feature. At all.

Natural History

In fact, it appears in the zoological writing of the ancient Greeks, because as far as they were concerned, the unicorn was a real animal. Whether or not it was a white horse with a horn is a different question, but we'll get to that later.

Instead, our unicorn 'myth' is the story of the maiden and the unicorn. Like most things to do with our horned friend, the facts are misty, but it seems that the story first appeared in writing around the second century AD in the *Physiologus*, a sort of moral guidebook compiled in Greek by an unknown author (or authors).

'So to follow the unicorn is to track one aspect of mankind's progress across 2500 years. It is a windy road with many charming vistas, and many strange ones.'

CHRIS LAVERS, *THE NATURAL HISTORY OF UNICORNS*

The Maiden and the Unicorn

The *Physiologus* tells various animal-related tales of antelopes, vipers, whales and other everyday critters, with a moral after each one relating it to the Christian faith. In amongst these are more fantastic beasts (although no instruction on where to find them), including the phoenix, the ant-lion (the front of a lion and back of an ant) and the unicorn.

The tale of the maiden and the unicorn is a simple one: a unicorn (usually described as a small but strong animal, somewhat goat-like) lives in the forest and no hunter can capture him. He's too fierce a fighter for that.

'"The unicorn", she said, "was a marvelous beast, shining with honor, wisdom and strength. Just to see him strengthened the soul."'

MEGAN LINDHOLM, *THE UNICORN IN THE MAZE*

Chaste Me

Instead they lead a virgin to him, and the unicorn immediately lies in her lap like a dog, at which point the hunters catch him and cart him off to the king's palace.

This story has gone on to form the foundation of unicorn lore in the West. Versions of it exist in languages including Greek, Arabic, Syriac (the language of ancient Syria), Latin, Icelandic, Italian and Anglo-Saxon. It's interpreted as symbolizing the life and death of Christ and his relationship with his mother, and also as an allegory for romantic love between man and woman. But it's not the only version of the story.

Unicorn Myths Around the World

The Indian epic *Mahabharata*, written down some time between 400 BC and AD 300 but probably told as stories long before then, also contains a remarkably similar story about a horned deity subdued by love for a pure woman and taken to the court of the king. Ancient writings from the civilizations of Iraq and Iran also include unicorns or unicorn-like creatures, while unicorn historian (yes, that's a thing) Odell

'The legs, so delicately shaped, balanced a body wrought of finest ivory. And as he moved, his coat shone like reflected moonlight. High on his forehead rose the magic horn, the sign of his uniqueness: a tower held upright by his alert, yet gentle, timid gait.'

RAINER MARIA RILKE, 'THE UNICORN'

Shepard (1884–1967) refers to a traditional African hunters' tale that bears striking similarities to the story of the maiden and the unicorn, in *The Lore of the Unicorn* (1930).

Asian Unicorns

Further East we find other unicorns. The Chinese had the horned 'qilin', a benevolent animal with a gentle nature that could see into the future, while in Japan the equivalent 'kirin' was calm and kind. Their looks varied: the qilin was a sort of horse/dragon/fish remix; the kirin, much more deer-like. Elsewhere, the cheerful Vietnamese unicorn is something of a chameleon and appears differently to different people, so might have deer's horns, or a dragon's head, or fish whiskers, depending on its mood (and yours). The Middle Eastern *karkadann* is less jolly, however, with a rhino-like appearance and a temper to match.

The First Story

In *The Natural History of Unicorns* (2009), Chris Lavers suggests that there's an even more ancient ancestor of all of these tales: *The Epic of Gilgamesh*. It's widely believed to be the earliest

surviving work of great literature – the clay tablets that the oldest complete version is written on date back to at least 1800 BC.

Part of the story talks about Enkidu, a wild man who cannot be tamed. That is, until Gilgamesh sends a woman to him, who subdues his crazy spirit and brings him to wisdom. Enkidu has no horn, but Lavers argues that maybe the essence of a unicorn isn't about how it looks.

The Old Man of the Forest

'Given the many similarities between Enkidu's experiences and those of the other unicorns we have encountered,' Lavers writes, 'perhaps we should pause to think whether chasing down the unicorn by its one horn and four legs is sensible.'

Instead, maybe the essence of a unicorn is in how it acts: a compassionate but wild being brought

peacefully into our world by its relationship with a woman. Lavers points out that this ties in with many Asian myths about the orang-utan, 'the old man of the forest'. So there we have it – one possible incarnation of the unicorn may in fact be a charming, orange-haired and gentle forest giant.

Modern Magic

What does this stew of origin myths tell us? It's a glimpse into the amazing complexity of human history and storytelling for one, showing how different tales managed to spread between different ancient cultures.

But there are also the even more intriguing prospects that those myths evolved separately and spontaneously; that it's human nature to be spellbound by the idea of a wild spirit and how it might be calmed; or that behind them all is One True Unicorn that once roamed all over the world and was captured in different ways by different cultures. We'll never know.

Spirited Away

Meanwhile, the mythical unicorn has left the pages of antiquity and in the modern age has attained spiritual status, with countless guides available to help us tap into the unseen unicorn energy all around us. They're even seen as near-angelic beings to some spiritual writers like Diana Cooper, author of *The Wonder of Unicorns* (2008).

As Cooper puts it, unicorns are 'pure white seventh dimensional horses who have returned to Earth for the first time since Atlantis to help us with our ascension. They are known as the purest of the pure and have qualities of love, peace, calm, gentleness, hope, majesty, caring, magic and mystery.'

Small as goats, with heads of dragons, as ancient as the written word and now inhabiting different spiritual planes … after thousands of years, we're still trying to find the unicorn and bring it back to our palace.

FAITH AND LEGEND

So how did we get from goats and dragons of the previous chapter to a beautiful white horse? The modern European unicorn owes a lot to Christianity in the Middle Ages for that one.

It all starts with the Bible, as you might expect, as for centuries the unicorn was mentioned in Christianity's holy book as an animal of great strength that was difficult to tame. As in: 'God brought him forth out of Egypt; he hath as it were the strength of an unicorn' (Numbers 24:8).

Finding the Unicorn

The unicorn gatecrashed the Bible thanks to a quirk of translation.

The original Biblical scriptures were written in Hebrew and referred to a horned animal called an aurochs – a huge, now-extinct ox – which the Hebrew writers knew as a re'em.

However, when scholars came to translate the Bible into Greek centuries later, they had never heard of a re'em. They needed another powerful, difficult, horned creature that they *had* heard of, and that their readers would recognize, to fill the gap. So they picked a one-horned, mighty animal mentioned in their ancient legends: the unicorn.

In fact, inclusion in the Bible (especially once it was translated into English in the seventeenth century) was the best possible marketing for the unicorn, as it would eventually sneak beyond its pages to find a wider audience amongst the writers, artists and poets who would take it from a case of mistaken identity – the unicorn for the aurochs – towards the modern beast that is very much its own animal.

Whoah, There

Eventually the confusion over the language was cleared up and the Bible now refers to an ox, not a unicorn.

The Unicorn Runs True

This early translation (from around 300–200 BC) became the basis for much of the Old Testament, so for hundreds of years as the Christian Bible spread across the West, unicorns roamed its pages. Along the way it became associated with Jesus, Mary and innocence, purity and sacrifice – qualities it would keep right up to the present day.

But the Christian unicorn presents another puzzle: how did the Greek translators know about it in the first place? And what made them think it was a wild, untameable beast that would be familiar to readers in their part of the world? The answers lie even further back in history with Greek scholars of the ancient world and their accounts of what they did on their holidays.

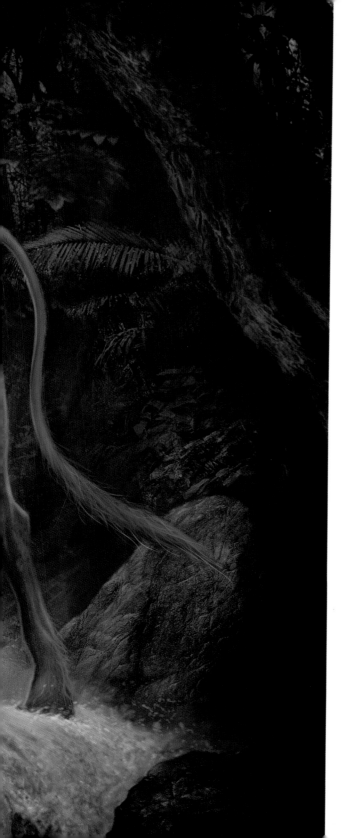

India!

For Europeans, India seems to have always had a mystical appeal – travellers continue to wander off there to find themselves, coming back with misty eyes and bangles and stories of elephants and cows in the road.

So it's probably not surprising that the continent held even more appeal to writers like Ctesias, a Greek historian of the fifth century BC, for whom India was an impossibly distant, mysterious realm. While journeying through Persia, he picked up accounts of a strange animal there (he never actually went to India himself), which he described in his book *Indica* as a wild ass with a horn, 'one of the strongest of all creatures. It defends itself with its horn, teeth, and hoofs, and slays many horses and men.' He also mentions that the horn is used to make protective potions, perhaps contributing to later myths about the healing powers of unicorn horn.

'Now I will believe that there are unicorns...'

WILLIAM SHAKESPEARE, *THE TEMPEST*

Later writers, including Greek philosopher Aristotle (384–22 BC) and Roman philosopher Pliny the Elder (AD 23–79), also wrote about fierce, one-horned creatures in far-flung parts of the globe to which they had never been – and probably referring to a copy of Ctesias while they were at it. Their versions were even wilder. In Pliny's words, there is 'a very fierce animal called the monoceros which has the head of the stag, the feet of the elephant, and the tail of the boar, while the rest of the body is like that of the horse' (*Natural History*).

Rambling On

These were accounts of natural history, detailing the 'real' world, so it's understandable that later scholars would take them at face value and write about the unicorn as a real animal, including those working on the translations of the Bible mentioned above.

So the fierce wild ass of the ancient world became the untameable one-horned beast of early versions of the Bible, and from there it nimbly leapt into the bizarre world of *Physiologus* and the tale of the unicorn and the maiden. Then it was a short hop of a few more centuries – nothing to a unicorn – into the Middle Ages.

Love and Other Animals

At this point the unicorn becomes the star of very different stories. On the one hand it features in bestiaries (illustrated volumes that described various animals) like the twelfth-century *Aberdeen Bestiary*. These were descendants of *Physiologus:* illustrated books that used animals to teach about Christian morality, as well as telling tall tales about various outlandish creatures.

On the other hand it became associated with courtly love, idealized romance and the codes of chivalry that were at the heart of royal courts at the time (there's more about this in the *War Horse* chapter, page 56). It featured in all

manner of poetry, and was adopted as a symbol by knights, where it rapidly became more and more horse-like, perhaps by association with the knights' own noble animals.

'But is the unicorn a falsehood? It's the sweetest of animals and a noble symbol. It stands for Christ and for chastity; it can be captured only by setting a virgin in the forest, so that the animal, catching her most chaste odor, will go and lay its head in her lap, offering itself as prey to the hunters' snares.'

UMBERTO ECO, *THE NAME OF THE ROSE*

India Again!

We're getting closer to 'our' unicorn. But let's take a quick detour, back to India in the early 1200s, for a strange encounter. Standing on a high mountain pass, looking down the land he had marched his army countless miles to conquer, the great Mongol leader Genghis Khan encountered an animal with one horn that bowed three times before him. As the legend goes, Khan took this animal to be the spirit of his father warning him not to proceed into the land of the Buddha, so he turned his army around and left India in peace.

The unicorn had saved India from conquest. But what's all the more astonishing is that the animal could have been real – as we'll discover in the next chapter.

> 'Of all the legendary animals of art, folklore and literature, the unicorn is the one with the greatest hold on our imaginations.'
>
> NANCY HATHAWAY, THE UNICORN

REAL UNICORNS

The unicorn of the ancient world probably wasn't conjured out of thin air. There's a very good chance that it was inspired by a living, breathing animal – or maybe a combination of them (a fantastical beast made up of a cocktail of different creatures is known as a 'chimera').

In other words, the unicorn wasn't originally imagined as a white horse with a single horn.

It has had various incarnations based on real-life animals, and the way they looked and behaved has contributed to the unicorn we know and love today.

Genghis Khan's Unicorn

One possible inspiration for the unicorn, and very likely the source of the legend of the one-horned animal

that bowed before Genghis Khan, is the Tibetan antelope, or chiru – actually a kind of goat. It lives in the Himalayas, the mountain range that borders India, so that certainly puts it in the right place.

The chiru has two long horns, but when seen from the side, appears to have just one. Combine this with the animal's shyness, meaning it's usually seen at a distance, and it's easy to see how it could be the basis of tales about a one-horned animal living in the mountains of Tibet.

Ctesias's Ass

In *The Natural History of Unicorns*, Chris Lavers suggests that the chiru, mixed with another Tibetan animal, could explain the ferocious Indian ass described by Ctesias (*see* page 33). The kiang, a real-life Tibetan ass, sets us off down the strong, horse-like animal track. It ticks many unicorn boxes: fierce, untameable, fast.

Mix them together (with a dash of yak and rhino) in folk tales and you have the origins of a powerful one-horned mythical animal. As Lavers puts it, 'the legend of the unicorn is far from being a tall tale.'

Did You Just Say Rhino?

Yes. The Indian rhino may have played its part in the Tibetan origins of the unicorn, according to Lavers, but the rhinoceros may have contributed much more widely to the unicorn story.

Different species of rhino once lived across Southeast Asia, Africa and even South America, sharing the world with early humans; perhaps they were the life models for ancient 'unicorn' cave art?

In more recent times, travellers (like thirteenth-century explorer Marco Polo) reporting 'unicorn' sightings added to the myth; they'd actually spotted rhinos.

Leinwen Jackson

'They have a single large black horn in the middle of the forehead…. They have a head like a wild boar's and always carry it stooped towards the ground. They spend their time wallowing in mud and slime. They are very ugly brutes to look at. They are not at all such as we describe them when we relate that they let themselves be captured by virgins.'

MARCO POLO DESCRIBES A 'UNICORN', ACTUALLY A JAVAN RHINOCEROS

The Sea Unicorn

If any animal deserves to be called the 'unicorn of the sea', it's the narwhal. It's a small Arctic whale, but with a twist: it has a giant horn. Well, actually a tooth. On male narwhals, it grows outwards from the upper lip and can be more than ten feet long.

Narwhal horns came to Europe with the Vikings and Danish sailors, and traders passed them off as 'unicorn' horns to make them more enticing. It was a good sales strategy that changed the unicorn world: the horns themselves became incredibly valuable, while the narwhal tusk helped standardize what a unicorn 'should' look like in art. The narwhal itself? Not so much.

Impalas and Imposters

The animal kingdom has many other contenders for 'Best Unicorn Impression', including the oryx and the eland – both kinds of antelope, both creatures that early travellers in the Middle East and Africa could have mistaken for unicorns.

And as you'd expect, humans have played their part, in some cases crafting the horns of livestock into a single horn. Going even further, the mischievous mayor of Magdeburg in Germany used fossilized mammoth and woolly rhino bones, plus a narwhal tusk, to create a 'unicorn' skeleton in 1663. It's proof that whatever the legends, we've always wanted to see unicorns for ourselves.

MEDICAL MARVELS

The desire to get our hands on pieces of unicorns was made clear by the passion for unicorn horn in the Middle Ages. This was more than whimsy: in the fourteenth century the Black Death, a kind of plague, killed anywhere between 75–200 million people; that's up to 60 per cent of the entire population of Europe at the time.

'It spread over all England,' wrote contemporary chronicler Geoffrey the Baker, 'and so wasted the people that scarce the tenth person of any sort was left alive.'

All About the Alicorn

Given this kind of pandemic peril (and the dirty water, and the contemporary habit

'*Following the unicorn path requires all the strength, patience and courage you can muster. Unicorns expect sacrifice from those who love them – and from those they love in return. But if your heart is bold and your spirit true, the rewards can be great indeed. Downright glorious, in fact.*'

BRUCE COVILLE,
A GLORY OF UNICORNS

of using poison to ward off your enemies), it's understandable if people were always on the lookout for new, potent medicines and antidotes. Step up, the unicorn.

Unicorn horn was known as 'alicorn', from the Italian word *alicorno* ('the horn') and was thought to have medicinal properties. As we know from the previous chapter it wasn't actually plucked from the head of a horned horse: an alicorn was actually the tusk of a narwhal, which came to be the accepted standard for alicorn in the Middle Ages.

Magical Medicine

Unicorn lore from around the world had long argued that the animal had magical healing powers, but by the fourteenth century these ideas began to solidify around something, well, solid: the alicorn. Here was a physical object that could be held, used and, of course, sold.

What did it actually do? Scholars held that it could cure plague, of course, or detect toxic substances and poisons, which made it appealing to paranoid royalty everywhere.

The Alicorn Cure-All

Alicorn duly popped up in dining rooms across the continent as the wealthy, suspicious nobility drank from alicorn cups, dipped alicorn in their food and drink, or just had it near them at meal times in order to either detect poison or purify their tasty treats.

Towards the sixteenth century it was widely held that alicorn would cure various ailments (it couldn't), sweat in the presence of poison (it didn't) and that the horn would purify water (it wouldn't). Going one step further, the Throne of Denmark in Copenhagen is made entirely of unicorns' horns (actually narwhal tusks).

'I found the hum of his computer rather soothing, but it was the complete lack of unicorn carcasses that really pulled the room together.'

DIANA PETERFREUND, *RAMPANT*

More Than Horns

Not that the horn was the only useful bit of the unicorn. According to one writer, the twelfth-century abbess and healer Saint Hildegard von Bingen, you could ward off all disease with a belt of unicorn skin, have healthy feet with unicorn shoes, or place a unicorn hoof under your plate to foil poisoners' plots. You would, of course, have to capture a unicorn first.

Needless to say, the horns became staggeringly valuable and complete specimens were usually the property of royalty, although their exact worth is hard to know.

Big Pharma

Contemporary accounts suggest a complete alicorn was worth 'half a city'; in 1553, the King of France's alicorn was valued at £20,000, but he may well have been boasting. There's disagreement over whether the British royal family's horn of Windsor was valued at £10,000 or £100,000.

Either way, alicorn was worth more than its weight in gold. All of which led to fake alicorn powder being sold to the masses (you could buy it in London as recently as 1741) and the birth of an illicit drugs trade that has continued to this day in the form of all kinds of fake pills and medicines. Unicorns themselves, however, stayed pure.

WAR HORSE

We've looked at the ancient unicorn and its real-life cousins. Now it's time to – carefully – talk about its temper. Despite its modern incarnation as a doe-eyed, peaceful being, unicorns have seen their fair share of combat and have been associated with warring nations, knights and all kinds of mythical rage.

Their reputation for being short-tempered even makes it into Shakespeare's plays. In *Timon of Athens* (1623), Act IV, Scene III, the bard writes 'wert thou the unicorn, pride and wrath would confound thee and make thine own self the conquest of thy fury'.

Calm Down

This is a reference to the unicorn's habit of charging at hunters in the forest, who step

'Towards noon we spotted an animal gazing down at us from a sterile mountain peak of red black rocks. Our guide stated that the animal must certainly be a unicorn, and he pointed out to us the single horn, which jutted from its forehead. With great caution we gazed back at this most noble creature, regretting it was no closer for us to examine.'

FRIAR FABER, 1438

aside so that the beast embeds its horn in a tree (this unfortunate habit also crops up in the tale of *The Valiant Little Tailor*, mentioned on page 94).

As Shakespeare hints, the unicorn's warlike fits of anger cause it to charge recklessly, so that it manages to defeat itself by becoming trapped, horn-first, in the trunk. But it's an action born of pride and courage, which might explain its appeal to another warlike figure.

All Knight Long

To a knight in the Middle Ages the idea of chivalry was an important one. Chivalric virtues – a kind of code of conduct for knights – wander freely between historical fact and fiction, much like the unicorn does, so the 'real' knight is hard to pin down. All the same, behaviour like honour, courage, piety, devotion and chastity were highly valued by both storybook and flesh-and-blood knights.

Small surprise then that the unicorn appealed to them, appearing on their seals and coats of arms. Unicorns are fearless and formidable in combat, but could also be gentle, romantic and devoted to their lovers; all fine, knightly qualities.

'The unicorn and the valiant-minded soldier are alike, which both contemn death, and rather they will be compelled to undergo any base servitude or bondage they will lose their lives.'

JOHN GUILLIM,
A DISPLAY OF HERALDRY

The Knight Stuff

In other parts of the world the unicorn also appealed to military types. The Chinese unicorn (or qilin), for example, has a very different appearance to its European cousin – it appears variously with a deer's body, dragon's head, fish scales and ox hooves, but always with a horn – yet it shares the same virtues of power, wisdom, harmony and virtue. Thanks to these traits, it was adopted as the symbol of military officials in the Imperial Court during the Qing dynasty, which ruled China from 1644 to 1912.

Scotland the Brave

The unicorn has also been an important part of heraldry (a system of symbols, images and mottoes originally worn on armour to identify the wearer in battle, but now mainly decorative) since the fifteenth century. Sometimes it would appear in chains, perhaps showing its tempestuous nature tamed; sometimes the chains would be broken, hinting that the creature was wild and free.

Most famously, the unicorn is the symbol for Scotland. Scottish kings originally carried two

unicorns on their coat of arms, to symbolize the proud spirit of the country and its willingness to die rather than be defeated.

All Together Now

Since the union of England and Scotland in 1707 the design has evolved, so that the unicorn shares the stage with the lion on the Royal Coat of Arms (and on the Canadian one, too, just to be a bit more international). There are some subtle differences though, hinting that Scotland's independent spirit and the struggle between lion and unicorn lives on: in the English version, only the lion is crowned; in the Scottish, both animals wear crowns.

It's another sign of the unicorn's amazing adaptability – as medieval knights, Shakespeare and the kings of Scotland all knew, if you wanted to look noble and strong, call on a unicorn.

ARTFUL CREATURES

nicorns have gifted us some wild and wonderful stories, but their power to entertain and inspire started somewhere else. Way before we had unicorns in writing, we had them in art. Every since humans have been making and sharing pictures, sculptures and more, the unicorn has appeared time and again, adding depth, beauty and symbolic meaning. Its journey through art is the next step towards becoming the magical being we know today.

Rocky Start

Typically, there's a delicious uncertainty around what the earliest examples of unicorn art are really showing, made all the more intriguing by the fact that we'll never know the answer.

The one thing that's certain is that on the walls of caves in Lascaux, France, are representations of hundreds of different kinds of animal: deer,

horses, bisons, bears. They were painted by our anonymous ancestors 15,000 years ago, and among them is a creature with a single horn. Could it be a 'real' unicorn, an animal that once walked the Earth?

A Tale of Two Horns

On the other hand, we could be looking at a two-horned antelope, which appears to only have one horn because the artist painted it from the side. It's a more rational explanation, although not as fun.

Either way, the image crops up over and over again. Seals (imprints made in clay using carved stone and other materials) from the Indus Valley Civilization, which existed over five thousand years ago in what is now parts of Afghanistan, Pakistan and India, clearly show a single-horned animal. So, too, do seals from the ancient city of Nineveh (now in modern-day Iraq). But again, both could be showing an animal with two horns in profile.

Weaving a Legend

After an ambiguous start on cave walls and seals, more recognizable images appeared as the unicorn myth travelled around the world.

Examples include illustrations of the 'unicorn' in the Bible – some dating back to the eleventh century – as well as the symbolic architecture of churches.

However, some of the most stunning artwork to feature unicorns comes in the form of tapestries. Many examples from the fifteenth and sixteenth centuries run with the religious theme, and function as items of devotion in their own right.

Divine Art

Typically they show Mary cradling a unicorn, the beast's head in her lap, as assorted angels and holy beings – and God, naturally – look on. Showing Christ's mother with the unicorn is designed to highlight her purity, using the medieval understanding of the animal as a being who could only be subdued by someone chaste.

The connection between the unicorn and faith in art endured during the Middle Ages and Renaissance, but also spread out to embrace some of the other customs and concerns of the age: romantic love, chivalry, courtly behaviour and worship of the female form. It led to some of the finest woven works ever produced.

'The unicorn binds other threads of the earth's natural history to our own. If the beast is to stand for anything in the modern world, it could do worse than stand for that.'

CHRIS LAVERS, THE NATURAL HISTORY OF UNICORNS

The Unicorn Tapestries

Fans of unicorns might not immediately be thrilled with the subject of the seven tapestries that make up *The Unicorn Tapestries* (or *The Hunt for the Unicorn*), given that it's all about chasing down and killing a unicorn, aided by hunting dogs. Spoiler alert, though: there's a happy ending.

The story and life of the tapestries themselves would be remarkable enough, even if they didn't feature our favourite mono-horned mythical creature. They were created between 1495 and 1505, probably in Brussels or Liège, but we don't know by whom, for whom, or why. The letters 'A' and 'E' are woven throughout, but no one knows what they mean.

'The unicorn was white, with hoofs of silver and graceful horn of pearl. … The eyes … were so sorrowful, lonely, gentle and nobly tragic, that they killed all other emotions except love.'

T.H. WHITE, *THE ONCE AND FUTURE KING*

Creation Myths

What we do know is that the resulting works, woven in dyed wool and silk (sometimes wrapped in silver), are widely regarded as the finest tapestries produced anywhere. Ever. There is nothing like them.

They hung in the home of the La Rochefoucauld family for centuries, but were looted during the French Revolution and – so the story goes – were later found covering sacks of potatoes, at which point they were returned to their rightful owners. John D. Rockefeller, Jr paid one million dollars for them in 1922, but now they're basically priceless.

A-Hunting We Will Go

All of this is before we even get to the work itself, which is a heady brew of Christian and secular images and symbolism. There's no one 'right' way of interpreting the story, as the scenes the weavers created fit many possible tales.

The seven panels are: 'The Start of the Hunt'; 'The Unicorn at the Fountain'; 'The Unicorn Attacked'; 'The Unicorn Defending Himself'; 'The Unicorn is Captured by the Virgin' (two fragments); 'The Unicorn Killed and Brought to the Castle'; and 'The Unicorn in Captivity'.

'Unicorns are loyal and devoted to those they love. ... By following in their footsteps, er, hoof prints, ... we can recognize true love ...'

SKYE ALEXANDER, *UNICORNS: THE MYTHS, LEGENDS AND LORE*

The titles tell the story pretty well: a group of huntsmen go after a unicorn. They find it, fight it, get taught a lesson in fighting by the unicorn before it's subdued (as always) by a virgin, at which point they kill it (boo) and drag it home to the castle (hiss), until in a final panel the unicorn is magically restored to life (hurrah!).

The story can be read as an allegory for Christ's capture, torment, death and resurrection. It also reads as a tale of true love (in the medieval sense) as the lover is overcome by the maiden and forgoes his warlike ways, content to be 'captured'.

poetic meaning, it would still be a beautiful, beguiling image.

The tapestries now hang in The Cloisters in New York, but crop up in various curious places: *The Last Unicorn* film (1982) was inspired in part by them.

Hanging Around

The Unicorn in Captivity tapestry also appears in the background in the films of *Harry Potter and the Half Blood Prince* (2009) and *Harry Potter and the Deathly Hallows Part II* (2011), adding rich mythical texture to the look and feel of the action.

Beyond the Weave

The final panel of the tapestries sees the unicorn in a garden, surrounded by flowers and splashed with pomegranate juice (a symbol of fertility) and wearing a thin *chaine d'amour* ('chain of love'), a symbol in those days for a heart that was bound to another. Even without the centuries of religious and non-religious

There are other celebrated unicorn tapestries. *The Lady and the Unicorn* series, also called *The Cluny Tapestries*, depicts a noblewoman with a lion and a unicorn, along with other animals and birds. Created around the same time as *The Unicorn Tapestries*, the six panels that make up the series symbolize our five senses – sight, hearing, taste, smell, touch – while the sixth could be about true love, or even the prospect of peace between England and Scotland.

Wooden Horse

Not that unicorn art is limited to tapestries –
far from it, as the works on these pages show.
Artists have tackled the unicorn in many ways,
and for many reasons.

One of the more iconic examples is the
illustration Dutch artist Erhard Reuwich
(1445–1505) produced in 1486 for Bernhard
von Breydenbach's book *A Journey into the
Holy Land*, which described a trip to Jerusalem.
It's believed to be the first-ever illustrated
travel book and the animals Breydenbach
described, and Reuwich drew, must have
seemed fantastical: a crocodile, camel and
unicorn (probably a case of mistaken identity
for an antelope or ibex) all appear.

*'In the heart of the forest a
unicorn is born. … Among
the silent spaces of the trees it
grows protected, nurtured.'*

JOSEPHINE BRADLEY, *IN PURSUIT OF THE UNICORN*

Unicorn Kidnappings?

Another woodcut artist, Albrecht Dürer (1471–1528), created an even more bizarre piece in 1516: *The Abduction of Proserpine on a Unicorn* is a wild, dark affair showing a naked horseman dragging away a naked woman on the back of a furious, snorting unicorn. Behind them the skies boil with clouds, while the beast itself is enormous, shaggy and ugly, its horn jagged like a hunting knife. Experts are uniformly puzzled as to what it all means, or what the source of the image is.

Born Again...

Throughout the history of art the unicorn has cantered into view as a symbol for everything from virginity to true love or the brute, muscular strength of dark imagination. Renaissance artists Luca Longhi (1507–80) and Domenichino (1581–1641) created *Lady and the Unicorn* and *The Maiden and the Unicorn* respectively, both using the animal to highlight the virtue of the female subjects.

Things were a little more sensual for the Romantic/Victorian artists. With *The Unicorns,* Gustave Moreau (1826–98) showed a group of women in various states of undress surrounded by the animals.

'There is something about riding a unicorn, for those people who still can, which is unlike any other experience: exhilarating, and intoxicating, and fine.'

NEIL GAIMAN, *STARDUST*

'The blood of a unicorn
will keep you alive, even
if you are an inch from
death, but at a terrible
price. You have slain
something pure and
defenceless to save yourself,
and you will have but
a half-life, a cursed life,
from the moment the blood
touches your lips.'

J.K. ROWLING, HARRY POTTER
AND THE PHILOSOPHER'S STONE

The Naked Truth

Moreau got around the social conventions
of his age (summary: no female nudity!
Not even a little bit!) by portraying naked
'goddesses', because it was fine for them to
have no clothes on.

Later fantasy artists like Boris Vallejo (b. 1941)
had no such problems, so their unicorns – by
this point definitely horses – walk straight out of a
swords-and-sorcery cosplay party, usually ridden
by absurdly muscled, scantily clad warriors,
more often than not punching dragons in the
face for good measure.

You want it darker? Fantasy master Frank Frazetta's
(1928–2010) *Death Dealer* (1973) shows a grim,
hellish and armoured being on a grim, hellish and
armoured unicorn. Or maybe a horse with armoured
spikes. We're not going close enough to check.

Modern Masters

Contemporary art still dances with unicorns.
Ruining everyone's childhood, Damien Hirst
(b.1965) put a horn on a pony and put the whole
lot in a tank of formaldehyde for *The Child's*

Dream (2008), while Thomas Woodruff's (b. 1959) *Beastie Variation, Sanguinic* (2009–10) and *Landscape Variation, Sanguinic* (2010–11) echo the earlier tapestry work to create lurid hypercoloured fantasias, where the unicorns appear to wear knitted armour. A unicorn even appeared in a Superman comic once, in the 1960s. And to think, all this started with a shadowy image on the wall of a cave.

'Unicorns are immortal. It is their nature to live alone in one place: usually a forest where there is a pool clear enough for them to see themselves – for they are a little vain, knowing themselves to be the most beautiful creatures in all the world, and magic besides.'

PETER S. BEAGLE, *THE LAST UNICORN*

'"Unicorns", I said. "Very dangerous. You go first."'

JIM BUTCHER, *SUMMER KNIGHT*

BOOKISH BEASTS

A longside its journey through art, the unicorn has for centuries been a recurring character in poems, plays, fables and stories, and remains an intriguing part of modern literature. It's these stories that have further added flesh to the bones of the modern beast.

Some of those exploits have gone on to be made into feature films (*see* page 104 onwards), based on novels such as J.K. Rowling's *Harry Potter and the Philosopher's Stone* (1997) or Neil Gaiman's *Stardust* (1999), but there are many more to be discovered on the page – some old, some new, some rather more odd than others.

A Knight's Tale

Unicorns appear in various stories about King Arthur, a mythical ruler of fifth-/sixth-century

Britain made famous through Geoffrey of Monmouth's not-all-that-accurate *The History of the Kings of Britain* (*c.* 1136), the French romances penned by Chrétien de Troyes (*c.* 1200), and Sir Thomas Mallory's *Le Morte d'Arthur* (*The Death of King Arthur*, 1485), among others.

In one lesser-known French tale (*Le Chevalier du Papegau*, *c.* 1300) Arthur finds himself stranded on a strange shore, at the foot of a huge tower. Eventually the tower's occupant, a dwarf, comes to speak to him and tells the tale of his own arrival on the shore.

Lost and Found

It goes like this: the dwarf was stranded by a wicked lord with his pregnant wife, who soon died in childbirth leaving him with an infant son whom he couldn't feed.

Searching the forest, he found a hollow beneath a tree that he intended to take shelter in, but on moving the leaves inside he uncovered unicorn foals. At that moment their mother arrived on the scene and the dwarf fled in terror, leaving his newborn son behind.

Returning later – presumably after collecting his 'Dad of the Year' award – the dwarf is astonished to find that the fearsome female unicorn has become wet nurse to his son and is suckling him alongside her foals.

The Best Pet

At the end of the story the son duly arrives, now a giant courtesy of nourishing unicorn milk, and with the unicorn by his side as a companion. It transpires that the dwarf, unicorn and son are now a curious sort of family, the unicorn hunting and killing boar in the forest for them and doting on the son as a dog would its master – reversing the usual idea of the male unicorn being smitten with a human female.

No such reversal in Sharan Newman's *Guinevere* (1981), which imagines a relationship between a unicorn and King Arthur's future queen.

First Knight

Riffing on the virgin/unicorn theme, Newman sees the unicorn as symbolizing both the courtly (platonic) love revered in medieval chivalry – where a knight would pledge himself to one

'*When a unicorn is slain, men have destroyed again the image of beauty that they seek.*'

NICHOLAS STUART GRAY,
GRIMBOLD'S OTHER WORLD

woman of the court – and the future queen's innocence and chastity. Needless to say, when the queen is married and loses her virginity, the unicorn dies.

More bad luck befalls the unicorn kind in T.H. White's novel *The Once and Future King* (written between 1938 and 1941; published in 1958), which features an episode where a trio of brotherly knights capture and kill a unicorn in the hope of pleasing their mother.

The Last Battle

She's less than thrilled, alas, the death of the beast echoing the death of magic and innocence in the real world, which was at that time recovering from the trauma of mechanized global conflict in the Second World War – preoccupations also shared by J.R.R. Tolkien and C.S. Lewis.

However, while Tolkien's imagined worlds in the high fantasy of *The Lord of the Rings* (1954) are filled with their share of magical creatures, we need to head to Lewis's Narnia to find unicorns. More specifically, it's the final book in *The Chronicles of Narnia*, *The Last Battle* (1956), which features a unicorn called Jewel.

All Things Must Pass

Set at the very end of the world of Narnia (which technically makes it a cheerful apocalypse tale for children in which *everyone dies*), the book sees the Christ-like Aslan the lion return to dispatch false prophets – a donkey in a lion suit, commanded by a talking ape, obviously – aided by various human children and Jewel.

Refusing to honour the prophets and their god, Jewel leads the charge into a climactic battle against the enemies of Aslan. Lewis draws on classic themes of the noble, pure beast, who can't be corrupted, even in the face of death.

Battle Beasts

Jewel isn't the only scrappy unicorn in literature. Far from it. Although our modern incarnations tend to be more placid, their ancestors were often fearsome, spirited creatures who weren't to be trifled with. Take the unicorn in the German

fairy tale *The Valiant Little Tailor*, as told by the Brothers Grimm in the nineteenth century. Far from a cuddly forest friend, it tries to impale the tailor but only succeeds in getting its horn stuck in a tree. The wily tailor then uses his capture of the beast to win the hand of the princess, of course.

The Lion and the Unicorn

The unicorn also has an age-old foe in the lion, their symbolic battles intertwined with history and heraldry on the coat of arms of the United Kingdom's royal family (*see* pages 62–63 for more on this). So ingrained is this rivalry in British history that it's the inspiration for a traditional nursery rhyme, *The Lion and the Unicorn:*

The lion and the unicorn
Were fighting for the crown
The lion beat the unicorn
All around the town.

Some gave them white bread,
And some gave them brown;
Some gave them plum cake
and drummed them out of town.

Crowning Glory

Taking this historic theme and running with it, some authors have included both the nursery rhyme and the enmity between these two powerful animals in their tales. Perhaps the most celebrated encounter is immortalized in Lewis Carroll's *Through the Looking Glass, and What Alice Found There* (1871), the sequel to *Alice's Adventures in Wonderland* (1865). Alice chances upon the lion and the unicorn fighting, as the rhyme suggests, over a golden crown. The problem is that the crown belongs to the White King, whom they both serve, so their fight is actually pointless and a bit absurd.

Who's the Monster?

In *Through the Looking Glass*, Carroll flips the usual 'unicorn encounter' by having the animal see Alice herself as the mythical monster, although the unicorn does promise to believe in her if she believes in it.

A showdown between a lion and a unicorn also appears in the novel version of *Stardust* (although not in the film, thanks to budget limitations). In the magical world of Faerie the protagonists stumble on the brawling animals as they fight over a crown, and our heroes save the unicorn by snatching it up and handing it to the lion, who slinks off into the forest.

Fix You

Our heroes Tristran and Yvaine then tend to the wounded unicorn – a deed it later repays with its own life when saving them from the witch-queen. In both cases, the unicorn – a magical, impossible creature – is a helpful signpost showing that we've entered worlds that are equally magical and impossible.

A different kind of broken unicorn – a glass one – features in Tennessee Williams' play *The Glass Menagerie* (1944). In its unbroken state it's the prized possession of Laura, and symbolizes her own strangeness: the unicorn

stands apart from other horses, as Laura stands apart from other people. The two are similarly pure, and similarly naïve.

Play On

A shadow falls when Laura dances with another character, Jim, who breaks the glass unicorn in the process. The shattering of the horn and the violence it hints at suggests Laura has been made 'normal', but has had that normality forced onto her – and that she (and her metaphorical innocence and chastity) has been ruined in the process.

Unicorns play memorable parts in these classic tales, but there's also an embarrassment of riches out there in the world of contemporary unicorn fiction. A good place to start is in Luster, the world of Bruce Coville's series of novels, *The Unicorn Chronicles* (1994 onwards).

Modern Fantasy

In Luster you'll meet dragons, unicorn royalty, a quest to save multiple worlds and a memorable villain, Beloved, who is both kept alive and constantly killed by the tip of a unicorn horn embedded in her heart.

It's the tip of the iceberg: you can also enjoy an appearance of *The Lion and the Unicorn* in *Batman: The Animated Series*, killer unicorns in Diana Peterfreund's novel series of the same name (2009 onwards; you can probably guess what they're about), and the brilliant, hilarious *Heavenly Nostrils* comic strips by Dana Simpson, collected in the *Phoebe and Her Unicorn* books (2014 onwards). It's like *Scott Pilgrim vs the World*, with added unicorn goodness.

Magical Muse

Whatever your tastes in literature, one thing is clear: the unicorn has always been an impressively adaptable muse for writers, instantly conjuring visions of fantastical lands, romance and otherworldliness simply by showing up.

Sometimes it's a character in the story itself, propelling the narrative and bringing the weight of all that glorious magical personality with it. Sometimes it's more symbolic, acting as a moral guide; sometimes it reflects a changing world; sometimes it symbolizes many of the struggles we face as we grow up. It's the hero, the purpose of the quest, the fragile glass trinket dripping with meaning. And sometimes it's a mad killer horse. But one thing is certain – literature would be a lot less interesting without it.

'If you see a unicorn in a dream or vision, it may tell you to keep the faith – don't give up. A unicorn could also advise you to be more gentle and kind. Encountering a unicorn might warn you to trust your intuition, not just your intellect.'

SKYE ALEXANDER, *THE SECRET POWER OF SPIRIT ANIMALS*

'There are in India certain
wild asses which are as large as
horses, and larger. Their bodies
are white, their heads dark red,
and their eyes dark blue.
They have a horn on the
forehead which is about a
foot and a half in length.'

CTESIAS OF CNIDUS, *INDICA*

SUPERSTARS OF THE SCREEN

Our quest has almost reached the present day, with the unicorn on the big screen. It's not surprising that unicorns make great movie stars. They have the same qualities that all the big names have: beauty, a slight strangeness to their look, a little bit of mystery and the ability to carry a story on their broad backs.

In some cases they're the main attraction, in others they're supporting roles. Either way, they tend to make a lasting impression when they arrive, sometimes leaving audiences with more questions than answers. Well, that's mythical beasts for you.

The Last Unicorn

Starting with a film in which a unicorn is the central character, this animated

feature was based on the novel of the same name
by Peter S. Beagle. Discovering that she is the last
of her kind, the ancient unicorn embarks on a quest
to discover what became of the others, facing
capture, magical beings and a demonic red bull
along the way.

As animated tales go, *The Last Unicorn* is no *Minions*:
there's little room for fun and frolics amidst all the dark
magic. The unicorn herself is even transformed into
a human female at one point, experiencing all our
frailties and emotions in the process.

Super Unicorn?

By curious coincidence, the Man of Steel
experienced the same human emotion and frailty
two years previously in *Superman II* (1980), but
unlike him, the unicorn ends the film both alone and
not alone. She saves her people but also suffers a
heartbreak that keeps her apart from them.

There wasn't so much gloom for *Unico*, the
1970s/80s manga/anime series from Japan,
which saw the titular heroine in trouble with
the gods for her crime of making all creatures
feel light-hearted and happy. Protected by the
West Wind and sometimes accompanied by
the Scottish Devil, Beezle, Unico's adventures

included battling a demonic Cow Skeleton and talking to the Trojan Horse. Unicorns do seem to have issues with mean cow beasts.

Heading to Hogwarts

The Last Unicorn is pretty faithful to the source novel, helped along by the fact that Beagle himself wrote the screenplay, and the film captures a lot of the strange, melancholic mood of his book. Other screen unicorns feature in films that are a little more cheery: *The White Pony* (1999) is a frothy, fun yarn about a girl who discovers that her uncle's horse is actually a powerful unicorn in hiding.

However, mostly our horned heroes and heroines have a tough time of it on screen. It certainly sucks to be a unicorn in *Harry Potter and the Philosopher's Stone* (2001).

Wizard Bad Luck

In the film based on J.K. Rowling's world-conquering novel, at least two unicorns meet their deaths at the hand of dark wizard Voldemort, who drinks their blood in order to preserve his life. Rowling's unicorns are very much in the classical mould, appearing as gentle, pure beings with

'The unicorn, through … not knowing how to control itself, for the love it bears to fair maidens forgets its ferocity and wildness; and laying aside all fear it will go up to a seated damsel and go to sleep in her lap…'

LEONARDO DA VINCI

healing powers. They feature throughout the *Harry Potter* series, their manes forming the core of some wands, but it's their brief appearances here that linger in the memory – wounded, bleeding silver in the moonlight, perfectly highlighting the kind of evil that Harry is facing. Who would want to kill a unicorn?

We Could Rule the World

In a word: everyone. At least that's how it appears in fantasy films. Murky cult movie *Legend* (1985) sees a hilariously young Tom Cruise battling to stop Darkness (a red chap with big old goat horns) destroying the world by killing the last remaining unicorns and taking their horns. Unloved at the time, it's become a bit of a classic since.

Meanwhile, the unicorn in *Stardust* (2007) lays down its life to protect the heroes – in Neil Gaiman's source novel it has an even rougher time, once again highlighting the evil present in the story.

Going Dark

Gaiman places his unicorn in the kind of gruesome fairy tale world the Brothers Grimm would recognize, rather than something more

'Unicorns can thrive anywhere that the heart and imagination are receptive to them.'

PAUL AND KARIN JOHNSGARD, *DRAGONS AND UNICORNS: A NATURAL HISTORY*

Disneyfied and colourful. Sticking to the shadows, there's not much colour and cheer to be found in *Blade Runner* (1982), from Ridley Scott, who also directed *Legend*.

A sci-fi noir that imagines Los Angeles in 2020 as a choked, neon-spattered hellscape where it always seems to rain, *Blade Runner* sees Harrison Ford's Deckard hunting replicants – human-like cyborgs who have gone astray. Unicorns feature throughout the film in dreams and – even more enigmatically – origami, hinting at beauty, frailty and the mystery of what it is to be 'human'. Caution: also contains weird owls and scary toys.

On the Small Screen

Unicorns aren't all about the glitz of Hollywood monster hits and rolling into the club with bling-draped horns. They've also been content to work on the small screen over the years (it's where all the serious parts are, darling), particularly when it meant getting a major role.

In the adventures of She-Ra (He-Man's twin sister), Spirit – a pretty cool talking horse – is transformed into an even more excellent winged unicorn, Swift Wind, when Princess Adora becomes She-Ra, Princess of Power. Wow, that's a whole lot of 80s.

By the Power of Grayskull!

Swift Wind can speak, communicate telepathically, has rainbow wings and is strong enough to move a planet's orbit. All He-Man got was a little cat that turned into a slightly bigger cat.

Meanwhile, *Dungeons and Dragons* featured the regular character Uni, the baby unicorn, throughout its run, as well as many of the grown-up beasts in the 'Valley of the Unicorns' episode. A magical inhabitant of the strange realm in which our heroes find themselves, Uni has limited magical powers – she's only young – including the ability to teleport. She's the companion of Bobby the Barbarian and speaks in a curious half-voice-half-bleat.

Music Videos

Appearance-wise, Uni is your classic mythical unicorn, only pint-sized: a demure little horned horse, in other words. Swift Wind, on the other hand, has definitely been at the paint pots – this was the era of Rainbow Brite, Care Bears and

My Little Ponies, after all – to end up looking pretty damn disco when called into action.

But however curious things got in She-Ra, some more recent unicorn incarnations have Swift Wind beaten for strangeness, hands down. Step forward, Lady Gaga (who else?) and the music video to 'Born This Way', which begins and ends with a unicorn rearing its head, scattering stardust as it does so.

Born This Way

Gaga taps into the unicorn's otherworldly appearance to underline her message of inclusivity – it doesn't matter what you look like, you carry magic with you.

Not to be outdone, Ke$ha's 'Blow' features unicorns in dinner jackets, a laser-gun fight, bullet holes that gush rainbows and the head of actor James Van Der Beek mounted on a plaque.

What any of this has to do with anything is anyone's guess, but the unicorn once again proves itself to be an adaptable beast. Whether it's sharing the screen with Tom Cruise, cavorting with Gaga or symbolizing the elusive nature of what it is (or isn't) to be human, it's as at home in black-tie regalia and sipping champagne as it is wandering the fields of ancient mythology.

UNICORNS, UPDATED

The version of the unicorn that glides in glorious, shimmering slow motion through the movies (and Gaga's videos) is more or less the modern archetype: the gallant white horse with the horn. But unicorns never stay still for long, so in recent years things have been changing again.

Maybe after all those years of wearing white, the unicorn fancied a new look. They've donned pink or rainbow coats, and are now cuddly, wide-eyed softies snuggling up to children. We're a long way from the murderous Indian ass Ctesias wrote about in the fifth century BC: even Barbie has her own unicorn. And some of them have wings.

The Wing Thing

Unicorn purists aren't keen on the Pegacorn – a mix of Pegasus and a unicorn – but it's not a modern invention.

Pliny the Elder mentioned them, as did the medieval bestiaries, so it shares a lot of the same cultural DNA as its flightless family member. The truth is, there's probably room for both, provided they play nicely.

What's perhaps more interesting is why we keep coming back to the unicorn, winged or not, when we've left so many other mythical beasts behind. You don't see Cerberus on many pencil cases.

Modern Unicorns

Unicorns, however, are universally loved. They're adored by fashion, embraced by stationers, and even inspire make-up colours (Unicorn Drool, anyone?) and techniques – embellishing your eyes with glittery eyeliner horns was one recent trend. With #TeamUnicorn they even became the totem animal of 'geek girl empowerment'.

Not content with that, unicorns appear in World of Warcraft, Pokémon and Magic: The Gathering cards, as well as on countless phone cases, stickers, t-shirts and tattooed bodies. Sometimes it's the sugar-sweet pink unicorn; sometimes it's the more classical one. Sometimes they're goofing around; sometimes they have a serious spiritual message.

'I am full of tears and hunger and the fear of death, although I cannot weep, and I want nothing, and I cannot die. I am not like the others now, for no unicorn was ever born who could regret, but I do. I regret.'

PETER S. BEAGLE, *THE LAST UNICORN*

Unicorns Forever

What's important is that they're still here, helping us to make sense of the world. You don't need to believe in a literal horned horse to benefit from the lessons of the unicorn: being true, having courage, loving with respect. Looking awesome. Occasionally impaling the bad guys when they deserve it. Perhaps we keep coming back to the unicorn because it still has something to say to us.

So yes, the world is full of unicorns, of all descriptions. They've changed before. They'll change again. But perhaps what we can learn from their magical history is that there is no 'right' unicorn – there's just the right unicorn for you. The great joy of life among the unicorns is finding it.

'Jewel was so gentle and soft of speech that, if you hadn't known, you would hardly have believed how fierce and terrible he could be in battle.'

C.S. LEWIS, *THE LAST BATTLE*

RESOURCES

Some essential bits of unicorn-related info and entertainment.

Read These

A Glory of Unicorns, Bruce Coville (2000)
A collection of unicorn fiction from the master
unicorn storyteller. See also *Into the Land of the
Unicorns* (1994) and others from the same author.

Phoebe and Her Unicorn, Dana Simpson
(2014) The best thing to happen to comic
unicorns since there were comic unicorns.
Bask in its awesomeness.

The Last Unicorn, Peter S. Beagle (1968)
Influential fantasy tale that's had a lot to do
with how we imagine unicorns today.

The Lore of the Unicorn, Odell Shepard (1930)
A charming, witty and sometimes brilliantly
sarcastic account of unicorn history, especially
the zoological and religious bits.

The Natural History of Unicorns, Chris Lavers
(2009) A comprehensive guide to the real
animals that have inspired the myth.

The Unicorn Tapestries, Margaret B. Freeman
(1976) More about the celebrated tapestries
now hanging in New York.

Unicorns: The Myths, Legends and Lore, Skye
Alexander (2015) An in-depth analysis of the
story of the unicorn in history and culture, with
a look at the more spiritual aspects as well.

Click These

brucecoville.com
gods-and-monsters.com
tchevalier.com/unicorn/tapestries
unicornsrule.com

Tweet These

@hevnostrils – Phoebe and her Unicorn
@petersbeagle

Watch These

Blade Runner (1982) Dark, violent, nightmarish sci-fi. With nice unicorns sometimes. Oh so dark.

Legend (1985) Cult fantasy oddness. Horns! Giant red dudes! Tiny Tom Cruise!

Stardust (2007) Light but fun adaptation of the novel. That great 'Rule the World' song is in it.

The Last Unicorn (1982) An animated version of the classic novel.

Bored? Search YouTube for 'Pink fluffy unicorns dancing on rainbows'. You'll stop being bored.

ACKNOWLEDGMENTS

Author Biographies

RUSS THORNE (author) is a journalist and author from the North of England. His previous books include investigations into zombies, fantasy art and the Mexican Day of the Dead. He once spotted two glowing white horses high in the Peruvian Andes where horses shouldn't have been, but they were too distant to reach; he has been curious about unicorns ever since.

REFFELIA (foreword) is a Portuguese professional artist and designer. She is known for her digital paintings inspired mostly by the fantasy genre, pop culture and fan art. Her work has been featured in projects for clients such as Started Hare LLC, Inner Kingdom Games, True Warriors, Konami Europe, Aggressive Impact LLC, and others. In 2011, she won first place for the best digital artwork for *Computer Art Magazine – Portuguese Edition*. One of her works was sold to the American Embassy in Portugal.

Picture Credits

Special thanks to all the artists who have contributed artwork to this book, in page order: © **Jonas Joedicke** 3 & 85, 93; © **Reffelia** 6; © **Jasmine Becket-Griffith** 10, 13; © **Anna Marine** 15 & 128, 16, 24, 27; © **Josephine Wall** 19, 21, 22; © **Ivan Kashubo** 25; © **Rebecca Sinz** 26; © **Patricia MacCarthy** 29; © **Eva Toker** 30; © **Ken Barthelmey** 32; © **Roman Roland Kuteynikov/www.acchiappasogni.org**, created for the game Le Notti di Nibirù RPG 34; © **Daenzar** 35, 40, 54, 63; © **Hayley Harber** 38; © **Ana Cruz** 41; © **Ceinwen L. Jackson** 42, 44; © **Annah Wootten-Pineles** 46; © **Milica Nedeljkovic** 49; © **Selina Fenech** 50, 52, 55, 58, 60, 61, 62, 78; © **Marcus Jones** 64; © **Sandara Tang** 65; © **Pat Brennan** 66; © **Svetlana Tigai** 69; © **ElXi-Ameyn** 72, 80 & front cover; © **Natalia Hlebnikova** 79; © **Kiri Østergaard Leonard / KiriLeonard.com** 83, 84, 88, 90, 98, 104; © **Julie Stone** 87, 95, 102, 112; © **Silvia Duran** 105, 109, 115; © **2017 AdrianChesterman.com** 106, 110, 117, 120; Photography: © **Viona ielegems**, Model: Jolien Rosanne, Post production: Chester Van Bommel 111; © **Lauren Kelly Small of Ginger Kelly Studio** 118, 121, 122, 125, 126.

Courtesy of **Shutterstock.com** and the following artists: olbor62 1 & 119, 14; Catmando 4, 31, 43, 92, 96; PsychoShadow 8, 48; Elle Arden Images 9, 56; 3DMI 11; Atelier Sommerland 16, 108; Melkor3D 37, 77; Bob Orsillo 47; Jozef Klopacka 57, 68 & 97; Jim Cumming 89; justdd 101; Marben 114. Courtesy of **The Metropolitan Museum of Art, New York** / Gift of John D. Rockefeller Jr., 1937 71, 73. Courtesy of **Bridgeman Images** / Musee National du Moyen Age et des Thermes de Cluny, Paris/Bridgeman Images 74, 75.